Many thanks to the staff and children at
Redlands Nursery and
The Little Red House Nursery
for their help and advice.

Copyright © 1996 De Agostini Editions Ltd
Illustrations copyright © 1996 Pierre Pratt

Edited by Anna McQuinn, designed by Sarah Godwin

First published in the United States in 1996 by
De Agostini Editions Ltd, 919 Third Avenue, New York, NY 10022

Distributed by Stewart, Tabori & Chang,
a division of U.S. Media Holdings, Inc., New York, NY

ISBN 1-899883-46-0
Library of Congress Catalog Card Number: 96-83075

Printed and bound in Italy

Pete's Puddles

Written by

Hannah Roche

Illustrated by

Pierre Pratt

LOOK!
My window is all
drippy! It's raining.

Mom says I can't play outside, so Sandra has come over and we are finger painting.

Sandra can paint very good flowers. I'm painting a sun and an airplane. It's a lot of fun!

Mom wants to go shopping,
so we're putting on coats
and boots.

I like looking at the puddles
but Mom keeps saying,
   "Hurry up!"
She doesn't like the rain.
I think it's great!

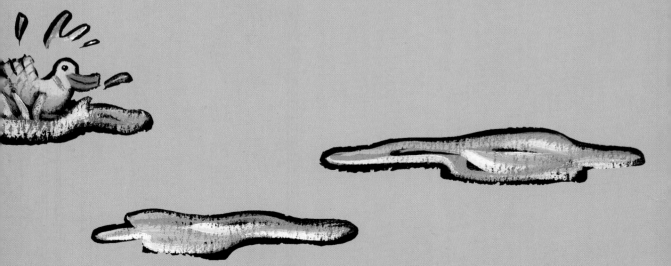

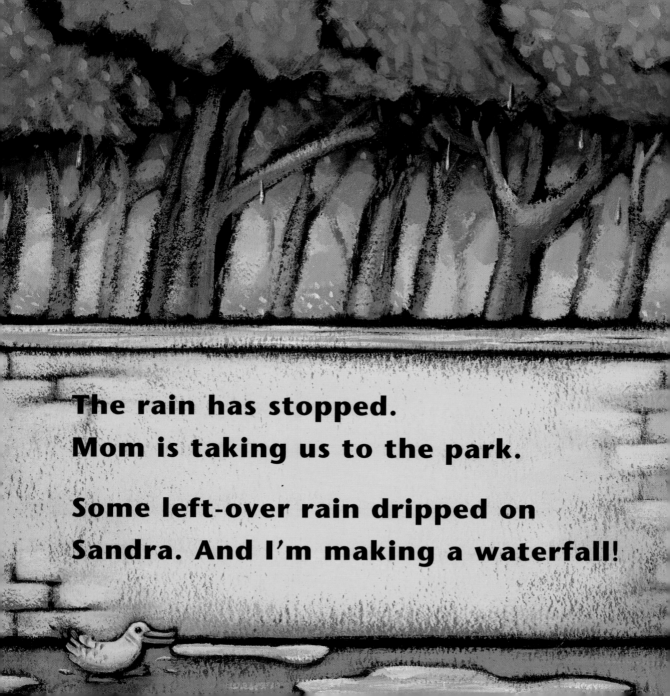

The rain has stopped.
Mom is taking us to the park.

Some left-over rain dripped on
Sandra. And I'm making a waterfall!

Mom says the slide
is too wet to go on.
But the swings are O.K.
if you sit on your hat.

WHEEE!

I love puddles!

We always have
hot chocolate
on rainy days.
Mom calls it
comfort food.